ĀNHAGA

ALSO BY JON FURBERG

Jonas

Prepositions for Remembrance Day

ANHAGA

Pray for Hardship

& Other Poems

by Jon Furberg

Smoking Lung Press / Arsenal Pulp Press

ANHAGA

PUBLISHED BY SMOKING LUNG PRESS

DISTRIBUTED BY ARSENAL PULP PRESS LTD

www.arsenalpulp.com
jonfurberg.tumblr.com

Library and Archives Canada Cataloguing in Publication
Furberg, Jon, 1944-1992
Anhaga : pray for hardship and other poems / Jon Furberg.
Co-published by: Arsenal Pulp Press.
ISBN 978-1-55152-430-6
I. Title.
PS8561.U89A53 2011 C811'.54 C2011-906294-1

ACKNOWLEDGEMENTS

Originally published by Arsenal Pulp Press in 1983. Some of these poems first appeared, in variant forms, in *3¢Pulp, Prism International* and *Writing*; others on broadsides co-published by William Hoffer and Pulp Press Book Publishers.

This edition is made possible by support from the City of Vancouver's 125th Anniversary Grants Program, the Office of Vancouver's Poet Laureate Brad Cran, and the participation of the Government of Canada.

PRINTED AND BOUND IN CANADA

ĀNHAGA

Hwale

A PREFACE

Stephen Osborne

The generation that came of age in the late nineteen-sixties came into no inheritance and no testament; they were provided instead with deception, evasion, prevarication and lies. The Past, in Canada at least, had always (that is to say, *by tradition*) been concealed from those coming next, hidden beneath layers of imperialist myth and the middle-class nostrums of a complacent academy, a lazy professoriat and a craven political class. The Past had been a secret for too long; those willing to take up their *uninheritance* undertook the required work of excavation: intellectuals and artists, dropouts, refuseniks, yippies, anarchists, feminists, gays, lesbians, Aboriginals, agitators, activists, women and children—among whom arose the poets, singers, private late-night ponderers, the publishers and organizers who undertook in myriad ways to discover, recover and re-invent the past, the pasts, that had been squelched, stomped on, flattened out, rendered invisible.

At the heart of the myth of a Canadian past lay the figure of the soldier-hero, a clean young man carried to heaven in the arms of angels. The language in which the past lay concealed, so well known amongst schoolchildren, derived from a platitudinous word hoard always ready to hand: *honour, courage, sacrifice, duty, loyalty, King, Queen, Crown, shock troops, valiant*. To dismantle this word hoard was to assist in reclaiming the language.

In 1971, Jon Furberg was a young poet of great talent who had abandoned graduate studies in English, and plunged instead into poetry and a study of Anglo Saxon—the language that preceded English—in a search for *what had been there before*; for more than a decade he pondered the song and the ancient lonely figure of the Wanderer, possibly the oldest sole survivor in the language. In the figure of the Wanderer abandoned on the battlefield, he felt a resonance with the reclaimed history of the grandfathers who had gone to war in 1914—an imperial adventure that claimed 60,000 Canadian lives; not one of the dead was brought home for burial: in a sense all of "our" dead were abandoned on foreign soil, to be memorialized in empty tombs scattered across the country.

The figure of Ānhaga that we behold in Furberg's rendering is the inverse of the soldier hero; his counterpart in the official rendering of Canada at war, as incarnated in Dr. McCrae's teary version of poppies blowing row on row in the breeze at Flanders Field, is the saintly warrior who "falls" in battle, and never dies.

The poems in this volume emerged from a ten-year engagement with the roots of language, and the roots of song and poetry; it brings us into the presence, the presence of mind, of the "anonymous speakers" of the past, whose bequest for future generations lay in the *wordhord*, the treasure of language itself. Over the years that Jon Furberg worked on these poems, drafts and rough passages appeared from time to time on the walls of the tiny publishing house of which he was a co-founder and editor, and in this way entered another word hoard in the discourse of literary publishing in the seventies. *Pray for hardship* became a working mantra at Pulp Press Book Publishers; and its slogan of defiance: *as for our enemies – leave them only their eyes, so they can weep!*

Furberg was a poet of great patience and humility: he made language his craft as well as his study and his medium. He was greatly respected by his peers and loved by his students; his poetry was sought out by lovers of great writing. *Anhaga* is his gift to the language that he treasured; it is also his monument.

NERTHUS

O Mother mighty form of night
Guard us in hell
In darkness shelter us

In the house of Doom
Dream us awakening
In the barren and sealed belly

O Mother drive us out
Of the throat of hell
Where we are eaten and broken

Great womb of night
Dark witness spell us
Out of hell jaw hell teeth

Bear us forth Mother
Strike us with breath
So we crawl and speak

Bring us the words
Unlock your loom
And wrap us in human cloth.

A FOREWORD

This book is a gathering of poems that emerged during an attempt to make a conventional translation of the Anglo-Saxon elegy, *The Wanderer.* Relying on notes, glossaries, dictionaries. etc., I pieced together a readable account, but it wasn't satisfying. Again and again, a word or phrase demanded more of me than what the scholarly apparatus provided. In time, my academic notions receded, as I began to listen more deeply to the words—words we would have known and spoken and memorized if we had been Anglo-Saxons living in England in 700 A.D. or so. I started thinking about the origins of this poem, and the anonymous speakers who, perhaps after centuries, had finally handed it over to some monkish scribe. And the sensation of the muse that such people might have felt.

I found myself embarked on a work not of translation, but of imagination and correspondence, since it was clear that the surfaces of modern English could not properly catch the spirit of the old poem without sounding artificial and anachronistic. The poem had become to me, by 1971, a species of literary ancestor, old words resounding with much of what the new words are grounded in. Images, echoes, etymologies, tones of voice—these popped out at me everywhere I tried to read about Anglo-Saxon poetry and culture to find out why 1 was not succeeding with my translation. Often I found that words which once had multiple meanings and shades of meaning could be tapped and offered anew only if one could recover a feeling for them and thus sense their resonances and implications. It was the speaker, as much as the event that needed an audience.

Thus, as I read the original, I found myself writing other poems—some of them translation, but others more ambiguously related to Ānhaga by virtue of only a phrase or even a single word, or a sound. It occurred to me that I was 'interpreting' the poem, trying to extend and confirm the original singer's utterance, no matter how much it might be apparently transformed.

Certainly, as translation these poems fail. Images, lines, passages are omitted at will; new poems are introduced without warning. Whole poems emerge from a single line, image, or word of the original, while other passages are verbatim. Some are treatments of poems that are historically later than Anhaga, while yet others imagine a time before. In this book I try to hear the experiences and the dreams of a forgotten poet, and to recite them afresh. Scholars have given us little sensation of the wanderer's experience, because they too frequently succumb to arguments about philological detail—thereby missing the generalities that are the source of poetry.

The language of the Anglo-Saxons in England—what little of it is recorded—is blunt and passionate. The dictionary makes it seem simple, as though one were reading a list of words in a 'dead' language. But Ānhaga's words are still alive in the roots of modern English. His words are very old; from time to time it is good to return to the ancient to recall the generation of our speech, and thus our meanings.

The compiler of a recent Anglo-Saxon word-list (Stephen A. Barney, *Word Hoard*, 1977) states that the vocabulary of Old English poetry is in the order of eight thousand words, of which most are compounds: a vocabulary of two thousand words will suffice to read most Anglo-Saxon poetry. Barney, almost comically, adds:

> If you want to compose alliterative poetry orally, first acquire a tongue-tip treasury of variants for the terms 'sea, battle, man, weapon, mind, treasure, distress, land, people and family, lord, to do, to say, to go, to know.'

To Barney's list might be added a few more words: *death, friend, exile, pleasure, honour* and *kill* (for which there are at least a dozen verbs in Anglo-Saxon). The wordhoard is the store of words the Anglo-Saxons preserved as their main inheritance, which they bequeathed to their successors as 'the greatest treasures of earth and heaven.' Such a restricted vocabulary, by its very repetitiousness and limitations, is powerful, because it offers a beginning made of the rudiments of experience—the elemental stuff that our language had already laid down in the boldest terms Old English could conceive. Ānhaga is the starting point.

He may be the oldest written European example of the sole survivor. In some battle—perhaps against indigenous Celts or else against another tribe of Germanic origin like his own—his fellowship has been wiped out. Instantly, he becomes an outcast, since his provider-lord is dead. Despite the arguments of memory and will, he is utterly forsaken. So far as I know, he, the 'Seafarer,' and the 'Wife' are the oldest solitaries in English literature. Barney's list holds true: the wanderer, who has previously known only benefit, reward, and gratitude can now envision nothing but banishment, hopelessness, and death. These are words and meanings which regularly occur throughout the text. Such nouns and corresponding verbs are principal among the clues not only to Anglo-Saxon sensibility but to that of our modern English speech; despite the contributions of Latin and French, Anglo-Saxon retained its key words, its vital hoard, to render human experience. In the poem at hand, for instance, to be 'walking the path of ruin' (of exile) is the worst possible experience—wretchedness.

In the British Isles, the Anglo-Saxons are upstarts, interlopers only beginning to invade in large numbers by C. 450 A.D., some 500 years after Julius Caesar had already claimed the island for Rome. Historically, their presence in 'England' is recent. These Germanic people brought with them a tradition of poetry, along with their other rites and social classifications. Poetry was their principal fine art, and it served an important political function: the poet/singer's job was often to exalt the heroism of the chief. By bestowing fame upon the lord of the community, he confirmed the lord's prestige and power; poetry had thus a unifying effect in its capacity to rally the people, especially the warriors, around a central figure. Poetry affirmed the nobility and tenure of kings, and a poet who could do this well was rewarded according to his performance. (England continues this tradition in the 'poet laureate,' whose main duty is to idealize the reigning monarch and advertise royal occasions.)

There was an historical purpose as well: alliterative verse is suitable for memorizing and so could be used as a vehicle for preserving the genealogies and deeds of warriors and kings—names, places, battles, who died, who lived, what became of them, and so forth. The great 'battle' poems, such as the 'Battle of Maldon,' and the opening passages of the Beowulf assert this aspect of Anglo-Saxon culture, wherein praising kings or other liege lords meant conferring historicity upon them, and thus yet another kind of power.

But it is hard to understand, in that context, why poems like *The Wanderer, The Wife's Lament, The Husband's Message* and *The Seafarer* should exist at all. Why would poets offer these poems in which the speaker is an outcast? Perhaps they were preserved as warnings against what might happen to someone forlorn, cut off from society, by implication showing what had to be defended at any cost; indeed much of the strength of the local community and its protectorate of fighters resided in the knowledge of all its members that to be separated from it was tantamount to hell. It was unlikely that another community would receive one in good conscience, since a leader was responsible for the past deeds of all who dwelt with him, as well as for their present acts. No one will take the wanderer in, and he knows it.

To the Christian scribes who took up the story in the 8th century or thereabouts, the answer was obvious: a man who is severed from a mortal king and false riches may yet find immortal and true ones. But one feels this story was told long before that moralism was added. And I suspect that long before the

Anglo-Saxons came to England, their poets had been singing of the special poignancy there might be in being left finally alone, homeless; so that one would have to totally reinvent the meaning of home or learn to forsake it entirely. Certainly it has to do with others, since our yearning for grace always anticipates the presence of others, but this fulfilment must be on some different ground, one the speaker cannot possibly describe, though he may well imagine it or hope for it. Surely that is worthy of a lyric and elegiac poem—the beginning, at least, of an answer that stretches down into the pity of suffering: down to where there are no kings.

The manuscript of the original contains interpolations in which the speaker suddenly sounds like Polonius or some hermit saint. These homiletic passages I retain, though in radically different form. Unlike Aeneas, the wanderer does not found a new dynasty; he does explore the rubble of the old a little, half-dazed, remarking upon this or that. His main devotion was fealty to his lord; since that is no longer possible, he has nothing but memory, and the facts of ruin, with which to make his life comprehensible. In this context, it is conceivable that he might discover, in his yearning, some sense of power and grace beyond the objects and social covenants for which all he has known have died.

The poem charmed me because all our poetry, I mean the poetry in English, started from here: in content, in rhythm, and in sound. Even though many of the words have been lost, enough remain to remember what is at stake. Such poems offer the audible sensation of a man's condition in circumstances we can all imagine, if only because we have dreamed them ourselves. Anglo-Saxon words contain that dream in which not only a story may be told, but wherein a poet's words may 'sing and say' again.

FEALTY

ĀNHAGA

Snow on the ground, yet roses
blooming—the cold, clear flower.
White heaven a hard waking to,
and the fallow jagged, frost-buckled.
Air ripe and cracking burns deep
in cut lungs.
                    Earth overcast with iron,
sky's forge steams and showers
ash into gawking eyes, slack mouths.
Felled horses still gout from flared
noses and ears—it thickens fast.

And all about, stunned and swollen,
the dead seem heavy clods in a field
gashed by feet and hooves;
shattered weapons stubble the furrows
—sparse, twisted harvest.

Yet these were men, spelled out of time.
split open, spilled dry, their hair
stuck to frosted stones.
                                        Go look
at their faces—all dead but you,
Wanderer, you alone, and only your skin
to enclose you—*Ānhaga*, the hawthorn.
wild, winter rose.

PRAY FOR HARDSHIP

Pray for hardship—
all earth's a common mound.
Dear Mother of night, I wake
and everywhere sharp-spiked stalks
drive mild flowers through the crust,
to stand pale in this cold.

In white hell, mercy might
be simple warmth, sweet flesh,
should abide as snowy petals lofted
in kind air. But here fragrant crown
shrivels, rosehips blacken,
stem and root wrung across the blown land,
a field watered with blood.

Then pray for hardship.
Who measures us?
Metudes miltse, Measurer's mercy.
Man, be kind—what if you woke
to find that all you know had died?

Before dawn they stiffen.
Gore and dung.
The hunters gone.
Nightcrows pluck at the carrion.
Eyes first to yield,
then the tongue.

ĀRE

freezing air pounds a door
made of skin. Nobody home.
Fingertips burned white, nipples.
ballocks shrunk to little stones.
Rain flays his skinny roof.

Lord of cold mercy! is this
your field? we are all fixed
in you, heaved up islands in low mist,
bloodsteam over the snow,
and ground too hard for graves.

Lord—your weather
glare of your old eyes!
Too cold for flies—
and all this meat!

WYRD

Walk the earth and it becomes
a sea, numbing and shoreless,
feet heavy as thought;
wade in deeper, pushing it back
arms become oars, hands blades
to make headway, break through
the ice, rake up the bottom muck

and out
into the expanse of waves,
heart weighted with memory
shouting a cry, words wrenched
from the throat—but the sea
sends them back again, whisper
from a dank wind, all sign
scattered, regions unmarked.

Wyrd, weird Fate, strange power
felt by those wrecked in time.
fully unspeakable, utterly. *Wyrd*
what happens, *Wyrd* what becomes,
Wyrd what is done—a man
scuffing and snapping through grass
until it is a sea. Cicadas
shrill among the ghosts of flowers.

WERGILD

First voice:
History stinks like a dead king—
sniff, sniff—you can smell it.
Friends roaring, sharing wine, boasting
of deeds—now they're rotting seaweed.
Their corpses well out of the mud
in cold copy of bitter slaughter.
What needs this? Who owns it?
Who cares for it? Birds scream in this
maze of cracked breasts and stopped sight.

Second voice:
What is the price of a man?
Snowy petals blown upon petals of snow.
They trouble the water as much
as the mindless wind.
Cloud, pour your clear wine
on their strange flesh.
Fallow soil drinks the bloodswill.
Soon, the sun'll steam 'em.
If the bees winter well,
they'll make fair honeyheads.

RUNE

Feoh, the first sign still.
Money, the first obedience:
goods, cattle, lands,
ornaments of silver and iron,
weapons, servants, slaves.
All property, and so all power
to give or to withhold.

Nothing spared.
Gold the unmeasured measure,
though many found Hell
is the greatest store!

For he who gave me rings
and torcs is dead—
I filled his mouth with proof.

Beneath the roof of a strange hall,
silence casts an oath to silence;
no one reads the rune an old hand
carves in a table sitting apart.
while all about the plates and cups
are full, and plenty laughs
long and certain to itself.

COME NIGHT

Come night, the dream brings them:
helpless horses, clanging steel,
deathshouts to Odin—Ēalā! Ēalā!
again I bury him, cloak him in stones
over and over.

Twilight calls me out to mourn,
and I do, though who can hear?
—all ears sealed like gates
in the walled town of sleep.

And then day swells, this wide unfolding,
as if the dead uncurled their winding shrouds
and walked in frail light, remembering.

What country is this? Is this
the country of the mad?
In the first hour, the hour of mist,
their shapes are meshed and tumbled.
world of small shadows, webbed words.

Braced against *Wyrd*, the stunned man
twists his knuckles white, squeezing time
into a seed—pain inside pain, king
and kingdom gone down into darkness.
Jaws locked shut, lungs knotted,
ribs tight as a closed coffin;
his thoughts rave, while his legs
send down roots into ice.

LINES 23*ff.*

. . . and so left there, wearing winter's rags
crawled beyond shore where the waves hurl
wall after wall mounting to crest,
then yield to deep amber troughs;
heart close-hauled against tide and tow
as sea floods and runs and turns again.
and Ocean only speaks to lift the froth
and spit white spume into the sky's whorl,
or growl and rumour with murmurings,
things unseen beneath, sounds mute-born.

Winds boil up the stinking wrack
coiling like guts in the blue light
and then towed down to maelstrom;
they draw at the tongue till lips crack
and lungs gasp, but the very air is rock.

EXILE

where he walks
sorrow keeps
steadfast and grim,
sole companion

path empty of travelers.
no bracelet of wrought gold
wound for his wrist;
nor any bloom of meadow
folded for his feet

his track is ever
through the freezing sea

FEALTY

Memory darkens his eyes ...
comrades burst into the hall, their voices
and laughing ring as they return, laden with goods,
sold and silver finely carved, gold-wrought tapestry,
good cloth and steel, all manner of booty,
and the great tables heaped with food, all of us
reckless and loud, the wine in large draughts,
all of us young and murderous, full of boasts
and shouting, and the best of us wrapped in yellow chains,
kneeling before our lord for new honours,
the singer swelling our deeds—those just done and those
yet to be done, promised by praises,
and dooms to our foes ...

then sadness and sleep,
    together, together,
come to accuse him again,
    sole survivor,
bind him in fetters of gold,

armbands and thighbands,
    hring on his hand
and gescy tō his fotum,
    chains of bronze

and they watch him approach the throne
and kneel as before, lay forehead on hand
and the hand on the knee in homage . . .
to dead fealty.

THE SWIMMERS

he yearns for his friends, and so
they come walking in the white mist,
the waves peopled with dim forms—
and he greets them, tearing the air
with beckoning and long cries . . .

but then, to awake—and see
only grey water, and some birds
floating there, yellow and pale,
spreading their feathers to preen;
squalling sleet, and snow mingled with hail
blur his sight. And they drift off,
dissolve without reply—
no human shout or familiar word—
just the low chatter of birds
to one another, or to the sea.

They swim away. The companions,
all the brave men—*Secga geseldan*
swimmath eft onweg—they swim away again.

SPARROW

TUMULUS

Look how they steal in on thin feet,
the wan, shrivelled ghosts grubbing the waste.
In the moaning wind, all wealth lies empty.

They are here everywhere,
heaping the midden anew, building the mound,
scratching their sign upon standing walls
hung with frost, houses abandoned, breathing ice.

These are the dead who still writhe,
spirits lost and seeking old doors;
they howl their names and the names of gods:
Tiw, quick to battle, mounting a horse of steel;
Thunor, whose hammer rings slaughter and tillage;
and *Odin* the wise, the singer of doom!

In crumbling winehalls, landlords and fighters
carouse in silence, dead and dreamless;
the whole host perished, backs to the wall.

MIDDEN YARD

I don't know for the world
why the soul does not darken
to remember them quick, and how
swiftly they fled—courage and strength
gone over to the far shore,
all mortal kindness sunk in hollow skull.

Eager for glory, we sought battle,
hoarding our fame, wearing our pride
more proudly than armour—
and when it walked it wore
a mask of rust, shield slung
on a bone arm.

In the last hour of light,
no thing stirs and rises, no form
against the sky goes humanly;
trees are lifeless sticks,
the cloud won't budge an inch.
Space takes the rubble in its claw,
things slip and shrink to make
an artless mass of weed and dust;
the sea lies sprawled along the cliff,
one darkness nudging another.

Each day weakens and sinks,
till earth is a tumulus—
mound of relics, dump of bone shards.
Death is the common father of our deeds.
We came and killed,
never learned to weep.

WĪS DŌM

no one knows more of doom—
the shape and bounds and mass
and course—knows aught of day's end
save he has eaten a share
of winter in the world

he stands beside the thoroughfare,
lets his heart cool and slow,
stays quiet in the sighing rain
which fills his bowl

doesn't cower; he stands
in the weather, face wind-dark,
raw hands, thick-skinned,
feet black and bare

no longer serves or fears,
wants for nothing, waits for
nothing anymore; he opens
his body's gate to the humble air

he makes no claim upon things;
the braggart broken in him,
lips quick to halt loose talk;
no claim against men—he stays
his own size; one false word
would take him down.

THE BROTHERHOOD

some were carried off,
dragged away

one, the birds bore aloft
over the high sea

one, a grey wolf
handed over to death

1 myself put another
to a shallow grave

HALL OF THE DEAD

Victory and loss are theirs—
theirs the blind ground,
theirs the still sand,
grumble of waves alone,
echo of past winds.
Trackless birds, their seed
whitens, all rage gone.
A thousand slain. Pathless men,
apparitions in pale sky.

Is theirs the honour in the iron
cloud ringed with light?
Is their sun a radiance
of souls and home of grace?
Theirs the land of wakefulness?
Theirs the storm of splendour
flooding the dome? Do they sit
to banquet in the city of friends?

THE WORK OF GIANTS

Lord and Shaper, so the dwelling
is laid waste; your people vanish
and the halls are hollow
without their clamour and music;
the ancient work of giants stays
        idle and desolate

stones they somehow dug and split,
dragged here, and heaved and raised
one by one, and set in weird shapes
to praise some long-forgotten power

a crazy garden of paths that end abrupt,
heavy slabs fallen, pillars askew,
worn by storm, pitted by the drill
of your elements, and only a few
still stand, propped against nothing
but the ordinary, bitter wind

they seem the frozen sweat of giants,
those who came before, and we
who no longer know or remember
have only the place of their labour,
can only imagine the fitting—
huge, and ugly, and complete.

Flowering Earth, who makes us
humankind raise our eyes—
there are no giants now,
just men and women, hands of mortal size.

THE SPARROW IN WINTER

for Meredith Thompson

She pierced the veil of blue silk
winter's wall—as though
a woman's water broke
and her babe fell
into the solid stubborn world

At the host's table we gorge;
women serve willingly
though we love little save war
and coming back to boast
and sleep upon them

Outside it rains and snows
air thin as milk; groundswells
heave the floor, roofbeams
creak under ice, earth tilts
and sullen thunders groan.

Comes a sparrow hopping to and fro
at the rim of no window
no window at all—no chimney
and no door—flings herself back

and forth, shudder of brightness
in the gloom, flash of a wing
in a drunk king's eye

Help us, O sparrow,
Help us look everywhere.
Life is long at the table of ghosts
where we sip from a wide dish
of dreams and pass it on—
wildmen's blood, blind wrath,
your own heart and tongue

Tell, frailest thing—
us old men wandering ruined day
who know dead beyond measure—
tell where the horses run
marrow and meadow, men and sons
gone down, no money, no empty chair
set before plenty!

You cut a sign on the close air
brush the rafter, wheel and shriek
thinking of an opening where the sun
slips seaward, low beams level
on the earth under glowing cloud

Winter calls you home, so fly
out the far door, sparrow, the hour
fly with you—slip under cover
of night—*swā hēo nō wære*—
as though this never were.

Your body was a kindly light
coming ashine into this hall,
you seemed the glimpse of very heaven
here scattering spark—and no one
to listen, none to see you fall.

THE WALL

Where friends once walked
stands a wondrous high wall
laced with serpent shapes,
as if their words were graved
in every crack:

"Power of weapons hungry for flesh
has swept us away. This is our glory."

Storms flail the stonecliffs,
thick snow binds the land—
the terrible sounds of winter.
Then come want and pallor,
night shadow darkens,
hail from the thunderhead
flung out of the North—
men driven before it.

All suffer. All is hardship.
The kingdom of earth is
Fate's heavy creature,
World under Heaven.

WHALE

ĒALĀ

Ēalā   Ēalā
Ēalā   the trembling cup
Ēalā   man made of flames
Ēalā   lordly people!

abundance soon passes,
friendship is fleeting;
no one may linger,
bloodbonds swiftly cut.
the whole substance stands
forlorn and silent

all creatures vanish,
a brief span for lovers
women and men—
time severs all.

Gladly would I watch you come,
but I walk up and down
and find you nowhere—
not in the deep or from the hill
not in the high cloud at dawn
nor on wide plains of sleep,
    though I search in dreams.
My shadow stretches up the far rise
    a senseless beast.

BLŌDMŌNATH

Arms and shoulders   carved with serpents,
waist girdled in bronze   beaten gold—
Odin who named all   healed none:
one knocked down   a spear in his eye.
one made to wear   a mantle of fire,
one a mere head   frowning in mud!

Odin the craftsman   red in the forgelight
raises his hammer   higher than doom
to flash upon   the shield of night:
one trying to run   away in the mist
stops to look down   nothing below his knees,
    dropped with a cry   to Odin the deaf,
    legs blunt stumps   like altar stones
    burned iron, cracked   and half-buried,
    but the animals heard,   hewed him down
    until he stared   straight into heave
    and the wild dog's ecstasy!

Odin the new field,   and the sower,
Odin the spoiled seed   the cry for water:
Odin the one pinned to a tree,   warped, ugly limb,
    the forest afire,   trees gnarled black,
    burls like warts,   deadfalls roiling
    in steaming muck,   nothing to glean;

here men are hardwood,   human bark
burns hot and long   smoke grey and sodden!

Men's tongues riddled   but the constant sea
is wide as god's eye;   She lifts and sighs:
Odin the long sun,   longer dark,
Odin the speechless   master of song,
Odin the reaper   and the gatherer:
Sky bulging and thundering,   bloodswath
through young, silver wheat   green hay.
One in a meadow   her thighs stained;
woman in labour   struck in her belly.
She is our harvest!

Bring in the weaklings   from all the stock.
It is the month of blood,   the air already
full of the North.   There will be feasting!
"As for our enemies,   we shall leave them .
only their eyes,   so they can weep."

NIGHTSPELL

Wounding words, whetted on flesh.
words of hooked steel, barbed hail,
sounds hooded and harmful

a word with a weapon in its hand,
a word that scars the air as it walks,
a word that wears a man's mask

word that flares and breaks,
word that blinds and disappears,
word that wakes and speaks,
    eats, drinks, works, shits,
    fucks, sleeps, and dies!

word that shakes and falls because
no god appears though heart
cry out to very emptiness!
as if there once had been a better
birthingplace than rock
washed by cold waves and mother gone—
all-mothering sea, self-stirring,
pounding forever, self-forgetting.

'Let there be a spell tonight—
a nightspell fit to make men moan
and dream of starving, dream of flight
sleepless with shame, until I come,
till Dawn spread her slow, bright stream
along the low and waking land and say,
Behold your dead.'

RIDDLE

When the fire-watcher sleeps
I tend the flame on the rock,
stoking the cinders;
I till the field long after
you have ceased to plough.

This Spring, hardy leaves show
green through thawing peat,
and moss cloaks the coal;
soon come broom and heather;
my lungs are full of their scent.

I saw you bury him; saw
how you placed the sword; saw
you digging with your hands
to cover him—but I alone
still keep watch, walking
back and forth across the field.
Many are here. I watch them all.

I brought these roses forth
in the snow; I plough fields
of snow, fields of grain and weed,
fields of rain, fields of trees,
fields of hills, fields of clouds
—I pleat them all.

I alone heard his last breath,
heard the last breath of them all;
when I speak, they speak again.
I come like a widow whispering
among the slain, the slain.

I am like a bird that draws
a line of disappearing light
across a cliff face.
Among those who weep, the only word
is loss. I've lost everything.

This is I, the taste of salt
when you stand overlooking the sea;
the cold finger curved around your wrist;
when you are full, the voice of emptiness.

CITY UNDER THE SNOW

When you die
you shall walk in the sky
on a shell of cloud—
air swollen, glowing,
neither night nor day
but twilight without form,
no motion save the snowing
deep and endless storm.

Far underfoot are trees,
peaks of mountains, seas,
and a city there,
a city under the snow.
Old houses, streets, towers
giants made of stones
broken where they fell
among the silver flowers—
frail old bones
beneath white hair.

Snow rings the air
like blood in your ears;
below your feet and thighs
the human fires burn no more;
beside a frozen sea
the giants turn and snore,
restless in their final sleep;
their breath is smoke and mist.

Above, no sun or moon,
yet snowlight plainly fills
the rushing, boundless space;
beneath, down years of frost,
you may yet hear a deep,
old echo from the grinding ice—
this place we built of flames,
war in the night, bad dreams
of loss, and fields too long fallow
and too late. Each day, more bite
to the wind; a little longer night.

MORNING SONG

I wake
before the light break,
show an eye
to the hung moon
and shake in youngish dawn,
gawk at birds'
squawking flight—
Ha! you carcass sniffers!
graverobbers! I'm your scarecrow!
arms flapping!

I hum
before the sun come,
suck the sweet
milk of grass-stalks
and dew to slake thirst,
chew the corn husks,
lily roots—
old solitary goat,
greeting day I loose my dung
where I please.

Hmmm—
the animal stirs,
farts and blinks,
and tries to think:
The fleas have wintered well.
Smell that musk
from those skulls
steaming in the ripe soil!
Bees mass to the honeyheads,
hums the wind.

The wreck of state?
and what did I eat?
Roses and snow.

OTHERS

Mist yields slowly to a slow sun,
and I to landsend, leaving no trace,
no footfall on the rockface;
wind sweeps the dinted dust away.

Others stumbled here, left no spoor
or spawn. The path is marked by merestones,
cairns piled against plague, towns charred
to powder, glass ground to sand.

Weird light, and the gulls flare white,
ribbon the sky, come into gusts
and settle on crooked pilings, rear up,
ruffle, hunch and shit, and lift off
sluggishly, skinning the water.

Sweep of an oar—for what shore?
the damned are everywhere, scratching
in the dark, hungry spirits in torn hides,
or animal naked dance grotesque
before a fire of overwhelming wrath.
Children squat hideous as starving dogs.

Rosehips and snow. Make peace
with the barrens and the whole
ghostly company. Make peace for the last.

ĒASTRE

who wears a white cloth spun of water
    wound about her

no torc of silver at throat or wrist
    no twisting gold

but a water sheath, bright rope of air
    coils around her

breast and thigh wrapped as though a slow stream
    curled over stones.

Upon the tripod, She is the fourth,
    the dolmen roof

to each one borne to the ground She is
    the veiled dome

of heaven, mantle of water, bolt
    of this alone,

and She shall be the fragrant door.

SPELL FOR BARREN GROUND

Ērce, Ērce, Ērce. Mother of Earth,
All-yielding, eternal power!
Bring us fields   fruitful and flourishing,
meat of the ground   bearing in measure:
silver tips, tall   stalks to the harvest,
wide crops of barley   white wheat
to the reaping   —all you may summon!

Lasting strength   and all who serve you,
scribe your circle   about this place,
rows of ripening vines   guard from wrong,
send away sickness   sprouts of malice
sown by men   who curse your soil—
let no twisting tongue   of woman or man
dispel your words.   So we walk and speak,
driving the plough forth   to the first furrow:

Be healed, *Folde*,   O Mother of peoples,
be whole and flowing,   fathom of God,
your meadow filled   with food for our want.
So we take ground   meal every grain
then bake a loaf   a palm breadth wide,
turn it under   the new-turned furrow,
And say:

Abundant field,   food for human kind,
wave of brightness,   blooming with bounty,
Thanks to you who owns   the holy name,
Shaper of skies   and our earthly dwelling,
Who fashioned this song   and formed us
growing things so each kind   come to good use.

THE HARVEST

Words of the harvest . . .
haul in the bursting nets!
bear in bundled fulness!
let weapons be buried—iron
locked away when She comes.

Baskets of fruit and tubers,
grain sheaves tall, and cornstalks
in young girls' arms, dark berries,
boys their hands full of wildflowers,
grapes to ward off winter in our blood.

Bring it in chanting! Light wind
clears the air, cutting the thickness,
carrying sweetness, scent of the garden,
down the long paths, broad roadways
clear-edged, crafted and carved!

Thus the long-standing cairns;
thus the whales whistle and click
striving in secret ways through mighty seas;
thus the birds shaping the sky—
ah, heron, wings blue in the sun,
your curved span breaks near the thunderhead!

thus the curtain of hail against the hill
as the great sun slips through
to light and sing us home.

THE WHALE

Now the fit moves again,
weaving fish and men, urging words
from what mind's mouth to sound
the whale. *Miclan hwale!*

Hard and fearsome to seafarers,
to all who go swinging out—
fyrnstræma gleflotan, rearing up
in the ocean fire—is *Fastitocalon.*

His hue is raw stone, worn
sandhills girdled by seaweed.
Men think they've sighted shore,
where nothing is, and make fast

rope in their high-stemmed ships—
sæmeæras, sea horses haltered
at seas' end—climb up complacent,
ships secure, left adrift.

Cast up offerings of the sea,
too weary to dream of danger,
they make wickiups; fires warm them,
minds sunk in ease, grateful for rest.

Then he feels how they swarm
and cling as though his spine
were home, his skin harbour. And when,
content with the weather, they enter

their shelters, he knows. At once
without sigh or shudder goes down—
boats and men hauled under tide
chained close to his huge form.

This is the ocean demon
who seals drowned ears with salt,
bears us spitted on his spear
through the endless passages of Hell.

THE GRAVE

This house was made for you before your birth;
before your mother laboured you, the earth
was marked, and left unturned till now—
how should we know how wide or far to plough.

But here we bring you where you shall reside.
See how the roof is not yet lifted high,
but measured out nearby an open door;
and there, beyond the threshold, is the floor

swept bare as new. So this is your abode:
there is no window; the walls are low;
a ceiling presses close upon your breast;
your sleep by dark and coolness is caressed.

It is a ruin newly made, of clay,
a roomless mansion without night or day,
where you must dream and wait eternity—
till then locked in with a once-turned key.

Now go to bed. Draw up this quilt of loam.
Now only lowly creatures find you home.
No lover asks where you have gone, no friend
to knock upon your doorpost and descend

to see how well you're housed and furnished then.
Light slips so sudden from your eyes—and hair
that is so curling fine, and long, and fair …
warm fingers shall not twine in it again.

GLOSSARY AND NOTES

Page 9. *Nerthus*: one of several Germanic Earth-Mother figures. Tacitus (c. 54-117 A.D.) gives an account of her, in *Germania*, as "driving in a wagon drawn by white kines and attended by a reverend priest. In the ordinary way the wagon stood in a sacred grove on an island in the ocean-draped with a cloth which only the priest, who could sense the presence of the goddess, was allowed to touch. While Nerthus was on her travels every place she visited was festive, peace reigned, and everything made of iron was locked away. When she tired of the society of men and returned to her island grove, the wagon, with its covering cloth, and even the goddess herself were washed clean in a secluded lake, the slaves who performed this service being afterwards drowned in order to beget mystery, terror, and a proper reluctance to inquire into the nature of a sight permitted only to the eyes of the dying."

Page 19. *Ānhaga*: the usual title of the Anglo-Saxon poem. The dictionaries translate it as 'wanderer,' but the parts suggest 'the haw,' the hawthorn or wild rose. One of the hardiest flowers.

Page 21. *Metudes miltse*: of the Measurer's mildness (mercy). Metud is one of the numerous epithets for God.

Page 22. *Āre*: honour, reward, favour. Before the wanderer himself begins to speak, he is introduced thus: *Oft him ānhaga āre gebideth.* often the wanderer seeks favour for himself—that is, respite from his condition of calamity and exile.

Page 23. *Wyrd*: hence our word *weird*. *Wyrd* was a demiurge, the Anglo-Saxon name for the primeval power of Fate. It meant something like the possible relation of an event to the larger pattern of history; when something important, fatal, is happening, we feel the weirdness of existence. Cognate with *wyrdan* (Ger. *warden*), to become.

Page 24. *Wergild*: literally, man-yield. The legal worth of a person. When an Anglo-Saxon man was killed under circumstances other than in the defense of his lord, his family, or his property, his relatives could exact compensation according to that man's *wergild*, a price determined by his social rank. Otherwise there could well ensue a blood-feud, a vendetta that might last for generations.

Page 25. *Feoh*. The Anglo-Saxons gave names to their runes, the letters, of their 29-character alphabet, or *futhark*. The first rune was *feoh*: wealth; the last was *Ēar*: the earth, and thus the grave. A torc is a neckband, armband, or bracelet-often of gold or silver—made usually by twisting the metal so the ornament could be sprung open at the ends.

Page 26. *Ēalā*. Three syllables of lull sound. A cry, a keening of bereavement, but not just a howl, the consonant giving the impression of a separate word. The modern English *Alas!* seems thin by comparison.

Page 30. Fealty was, to the Anglo-Saxons, the principal virtue. In *Germania*, Tacitus describes the devotion of a warrior to his liege-lord: "For a companion to leave the battlefield alive after his chieftain has been killed means lifelong infamy and reproach .... A German would rather challenge a foe and be wounded than plough the land and patiently await its annual harvest. He thinks it is gutless and lazy to acquire by the sweat of his brow what can be won by bloodshed."

Far from being confederacies, the Anglo-Saxon and related tribes organized themselves and acted in small units, settling in groups as large as could reasonably be sustained by the land they immediately occupied—small fiefdoms. A chief was responsible for protecting and providing for those within his community. The strongest men made up his coterie of bodyguards: this brotherhood, usually called a *comitatus* by historians, or a sodality by anthropologists, constituted the primitive aristocracy of the Anglo-Saxons. The strongest became the richest, rewarded ceremoniously by the chieftain in their beerhall with property of various kinds. Thus the group of warriors achieved some measure of solidarity. This aspect of the Anglo-Saxon insistence upon absolute commitment and fearlessness in the face of death is given account in many poems, notably in *Beowulf* and *The Battle of Maldon*. The work that did not have to do with raiding, warring, plunder, or the ilk, was done by women, slaves, children, and weaklings.

The italicized lines are from 'The Prodigal Son' in the West Saxon Gospels: put 'rings on his hands and shoes on his feet . . . '

The Anglo-Saxon words in this poem are translated immediately before or after they are given.

Page 35. The italicized names are those of the main male deities of the Anglo-Saxons. Their counterparts exist throughout Nordic cultures. We still hear echoes of them in the days of the week: Tuesday, Thursday, and Wednesday respectively.

Page 36. Midden Yard. The Anglo-Saxon term for the world is *Middangeard* (pron. midden-yard). That is, middle-earth—half way between heaven and hell. I like the pun on midden, a refuse heap. A tumulus is a burial mound, an often huge heap of earth covering a burial chamber, or perhaps a common grave where many were buried together quickly, as during a war. Among the Celts and Teutons, this was one of several forms of inhumation.

Page 38. *Wīs dōm*. The Anglo-Saxon word is broken to show its parts. Someone who knows fate (doom) is wise.

Page 41. The hall of the dead is Valhalla, a common ideal among Nordic and Teutonic tribes. A place promised to warriors who died valiantly in battle, where they could converse with Odin and hear their legend sung. It is comprehensible that a culture that lived by struggle and war should expect to see their virtues glorified by the gods, the afterlife being a fulfilment, rather than a contradiction, of all that their lives embraced.

Page 42. Giants. The remarkable word *ent* (giant) occurs but seldom in Anglo-Saxon poetry. When those tribes invaded Britain, they found monuments and roads of the Romans fallen into disrepair, the Celtic circles such as Stonehenge, and the huge pre-historic mounds. Having no similar technology, they sometimes spoke of their predecessors as titans.

Shaper is *Scyppend*, the Creator. Another name of God.

Page 47. The wall. This poem is, in its entirety, quite close to the original.

Page 52. *Blodmonath*. The month of blood. November, winter coming. Kill the weakest stock, since they won't survive. Thus, a feast. Anglo-Saxon poetry gives the general impression that for several hundred years it was perpetual November in Britain, as though the poets anticipated an ice age. The final quotation is from Bismarck, c. 1870.

Page 54. Nightspell. Related to our idea of spelling—the right runes in the right order. One who knows how to spell possesses magical powers. The Anglo-Saxons believed that eloquence generated force beyond physical strength, and charms were serious invocations. By chanting from a high place, a priest might dumbfound and incapacitate an enemy. A spell could be made either to cause or to prevent harm.

Page 56. Riddle. The Anglo-Saxons composed many riddles of which some hundred are extant. They were used mainly for pedagogical purposes, and usually have obvious answers, I felt that Anhaga itself was a riddle, and have tried to make a poem of that—something a bit more enigmatic.

Page 58. City. The ice-age has come. Someone barely alive imagines someone who has died and thus escaped such a fate.

Page 63. *Ēastre.* Hence, our Easter—goddess of Spring and renewal. A dolmen usually consisted of three upright stones supporting a wide stone slab for a roof—all of this was a grave marker.

Page 64. *Ērce*: yet another appellation for the Earth goddess. A Ceres figure here. *Folde*, too, is a goddess of the fruitful land—the ground or meadow which, having been folded, will bear a harvest. The pagan Anglo-Saxons believed that infertile land had been bewitched by spells. This poem is a counter-spell, part of a longer ritual from an Anglo-Saxon charm.

Page 68. *Miclan hwale:* great whale. (The Scots still preserve *mickle.*) This is the strongest of the three entries in the Anglo-Saxon bestiary, or *physiologus*. Monks, imitating Roman models, told animal fables to present moral truths. In this case, the deceitful beast feigns to be an island where mariners imagine safe harbour; when they land, he drags them down. The

Christian interpolations are omitted; the rest is mostly given here. (If the word *wickiup* startles anyone, I can only say that it startled me to discover that the Anglo-Saxon word for building a shelter was *gewickian*.) In any event, these people were beset on all sides by demons, ghouls, elves, ogres, giants, goblins, monsters, and other grotesque beasts. Before and after the Christian period, these were the images of the spiritual enemy.

Page 70. The Grave. A poem usually assigned to the ninth or tenth century. Here I have stuck to the original throughout, but put it into regular verse.

JON FURBERG was born in Vancouver in 1944. For many years he was closely associated with Pulp Press (now Arsenal Pulp Press), a literary publishing house established in 1971, of which he was a co-founder and editor. His first volume of poetry, *Jonas*, appeared in 1972. *Prepositions for Remembrance Day* appeared in 1981. The first edition of *Anhaga* appeared in 1983. He was a revered teacher of writing and literature at Langara College in Vancouver. Jon Furberg died in December, 1992. Commentary on his work can be found at www.jonfurberg.tumblr.com

STEPHEN OSBORNE is co-founder and publisher of *Geist* magazine, and co-founder of Arsenal Pulp Press Book Publishers. He keeps a blog at www.waysofpublishing.com.

For copies of *Anhaga*, visit
www.arsenalpulp.com

For commentary on the work of Jon Furberg. visit
www.jonfurberg.tumblr.com